what do we know about the celts?

hazel mary martell

PETER BEDRICK BOOKS

NEW YORK

First American edition published in 1993 by

Peter Bedrick Books
2112 Broadway
New York, NY 10023

© 1993 Simon & Schuster Young Books

Library of Congress Cataloging-in-Publication Data
Martell, Hazel.
   What do we know about the Celts?/
   Hazel Mary Martell. – 1st American ed.
   Includes index.
   Summary: Provides information about the
   history, daily life, social structure, and
   culture of the Celts.
   ISBN 0-87226-363-0
   1. Celts – Juvenile literature. [1. Celts.] I. Title.
   D70.M376   1993
936.4 – oc20   92–43864
                                       CIP
                                        AC

Illustrator: Rob Shone

Design: David West
          Children's Book Design

Commissioning editor: Debbie Fox

Copy editor: Jayne Booth

Picture research: Val Mulcahy

Photograph acknowledgements:
Front Cover: C.M. Dixon; Ancient Art & Architecture Collection, page 33b; Ashmolean Museum, Oxford, page 15b; Bernisches Historisches Museum, Bern, Switzerland, page 15t, 25b; Bompiani Editore, page 35t; British Library, page 37b; British Museum, pages 8t, 12r, 13t, 14, 19b, 22, 23l, 24t, 24b, 27t, 28, 30, 32, 35b, 41l, 41r; C.M. Dixon, page 16; English Heritage Photo Library, pages 17l, 33t, 42; Robert Harding Picture Library/ Michael Jenner, pages 18t, 29b; Michael Holford, page 43t; Irish Tourist Board, page 43b; Magnum/Erich Lessing, pages 9, 13b, 17r, 19t, 20 , 20r, 25t; Manchester Museum, page 21; Musée Calvet, Avignon, pages 37t, 40; Nationalmuseet, Copenhagen, endpapers, page 26; National Museum of Ireland, page 39l; National Museums of Scotland, page 27b; Scala, page 8b; Staatliche Museeu Preußisher, Kulturbesitz, Berlin, page 34 (Ingrid Geske); The Board of Trinity College, Dublin, page 36; Unichrome (Bath) Ltd, page 29t; Werner Forman Archive, pages 12l, 18b, 23r, 39r; Wurttembergisches Landesmuseum, Stuttgart, pages 30/31, 38/39.

Typeset by : Goodfellow & Egan, Cambridge

Printed and bound in Hong Kong by: Paramount Printing Group

Endpapers: This silver panel is part of a cauldron that was found at Gundestrop in Denmark. It shows a procession of Celts blowing their war-trumpets, or carnyxes. The end of each horn is shaped like a boar's head. To the Celts this was a symbol of war and death, as well as of feasting. The cauldron was probably made in eastern Europe late in the second century BC. It was found in pieces in a bog and was probably put there as an offering to the gods.

· CONTENTS ·

WHO·WERE·THE·CELTS?

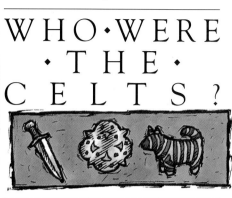

The Celts were a people who lived in parts of Europe from the eighth century BC to the middle of the first century AD. The Greeks knew them as the Keltoi, while the Romans called them Gauls. They are first known of in the Hallstatt region of Austria where they mined and traded salt. If you look at the map opposite, you will see how they spread out from there to other parts of Europe, including northern Italy, Spain, France and Britain.

THE DYING GAUL

We can build up a picture of what the Celts looked like from many different sources. These include images made in metal by Celtic craftworkers and used to decorate various objects. We can also read about what they looked like in books written by the Romans who eventually defeated them. However, some of the best clues to what the Celts looked like are found in statues like this one in Rome. It is part of a series to celebrate one of the Roman victories over the Celts.

METALWORKERS

Before the time of the Celts, bronze was the only metal known in Europe for making tools and weapons. Bronze was made from a mixture of tin and copper, but both these metals were quite rare. This meant that not many tools and weapons could be made. The Celts, however, knew how to turn iron ore into metal. As iron ore was plentiful, this meant that they could have many more metal tools and weapons. Celtic metalworkers also used gold, silver and bronze to decorate special weapons, like the dagger and sheath in this photograph.

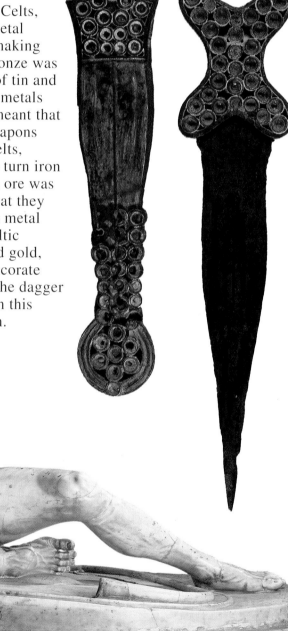

HALLSTATT AND LA TENE

Archaeologists divide Celtic times into two periods. The first covers the years from 750 to 450 BC. It is called Hallstatt after the area of Austria where the Celts were first known. The second covers the years from 450 BC to around AD 50. It is called La Tene after a settlement on the shores of Lake Neuchâtel in Switzerland. Excavations show that it was probably a trading center. As this photograph shows, the site is now under water, but in Celtic times it was on dry land.

THE CELTIC WORLD

Because the Celts had better farming tools than the people who lived before them, they were able to grow more food and so their population began to increase. They started to spread out across Europe, looking for land where they could settle down and farm. Other Celts became mercenary soldiers in other people's armies. Although the different groups of Celts had a lot in common, they were never governed by one ruler. Instead, they remained in separate tribes, like those shown on this map of Britain.

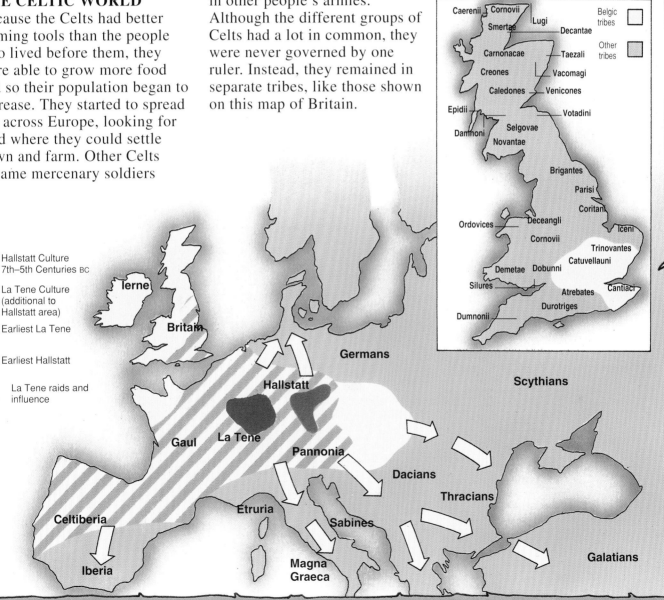

Caerenii
Cornovii
Smertae
Lugi
Decantae
Carnonacae
Taezali
Creones
Vacomagi
Caledones
Venicones
Epidii
Votadini
Damnoni
Selgovae
Novantae
Brigantes
Parisi
Coritani
Ordovices
Deceangli
Iceni
Cornovii
Trinovantes
Catuvellauni
Demetae
Dobunni
Silures
Cantiaci
Atrebates
Durotriges
Dumnonii

Belgic tribes

Other tribes

Hallstatt Culture 7th–5th Centuries BC

La Tene Culture (additional to Hallstatt area)

Earliest La Tene

Earliest Hallstatt

La Tene raids and influence

Ierne
Britain
Germans
Scythians
Hallstatt
Gaul
La Tene
Pannonia
Dacians
Thracians
Etruria
Sabines
Galatians
Celtiberia
Iberia
Magna Graeca

TIMELINE

	800–500 BC	500–300 BC	300–250 BC	250–200 BC	200–100 BC
IN CENTRAL EUROPE	The earliest known Celtic civilization developed at Hallstatt in Austria from around 750. The civilization spreads out from here along the Rhine and Danube rivers.	The Celtic civilization known as La Tene develops on the shores of Lake Neuchâtel in Switzerland from 500 onwards. Some Celts move east as far as the Carpathian mountains by 358.	In the east Celts start to settle in Moravia around 300. By 298 they have conquered Thrace and made it into a Celtic kingdom.	In 218 local Celtic tribes help to guide Hannibal's army through the Alps. About half of his army is made up of Celts. Another 10,000 Celts join him in Cisalpine Gaul in his war against Rome.	
IN WESTERN EUROPE	By the sixth century there are expanding Celtic settlements in France, Spain, Belgium and the British Isles.				In 198 the Romans set out to conquer Gaul, starting with Cisalpine Gaul. By 122 the Romans have also conquered Transalpine Gaul.
IN SOUTHERN EUROPE	According to legend, Rome is founded by Romulus in 753. Celts start to settle in the Po valley of northern Italy in the sixth century.	In Italy the Celts defeat the Etruscans near Ticino around 474. Between 390 and 387 the Celts defeat the Roman army and attack Rome, but fail to capture the city.	Around 300 the Celts make an alliance with the Etruscans to fight against Roman expansion. Another Celtic army goes into Greece and attacks the Oracle at Delphi.	In 225 the Celts are defeated by the Romans at the battle of Telamon. In 224 the Romans invade Cisalpine Gaul.	The Romans take control of Spain in 197. From 190 onwards there are many Celtic uprisings against Roman rule in Spain.
EVENTS AROUND THE WORLD	In 521 Darius the Great becomes ruler of the Persian Empire.	Carthage controls the western Mediterranean from North Africa.	In 278 20,000 Celtic families move to Asia Minor to serve Nicomedes of Bithynia against the Syrians. In 277, 4,000 Celts go to Egypt as mercenaries for Ptolemy II.	In 237 Carthage begins to expand its empire into Spain, by conquering Celtic territory there. In 216 Rome begins to defeat the Carthaginians in Spain, driving them out by 206.	In 146 the Romans conquer North Africa and Greece.

Romulus and Remus

Bronze plaque

Persian carving

100–50 BC	50–0	AD 0–100	AD 100–400	AD 400–
In 60 32,000 Celts leave Bohemia to join the Helvetii Celts, in Austria and Switzerland. In 58 the Helvetii plan to go west to escape attacks from German tribes in the north-east and Romans in south-east.		By 74 all the former Celtic territory in Central Europe is under Roman rule.	The Age of Migrations starts in this period as peoples from Asia and eastern Europe start to move westwards.	The Age of Migrations continues.
In 58 Julius Caesar begins to conquer Gaul itself. Between 55 and 54 he plans and carries out an invasion of Britain, but later withdraws.	From 50 onwards, more of the Belgae Celts settle in southern Britain.	Claudius of Rome orders the invasion of Britain in 43.	In 122 the Romans build Hadrian's Wall. It stretches from the Tyne to the Solway and separates Celtic Britain to the north from Roman Britain to the south.	The Roman legions leave Britain in the 5th century. South-east Britain is invaded by Angles, Frisians, Jutes and Saxons. Celtic civilization continues in Ireland, Scotland, Wales and Cornwall.
In 93 the Romans finally subdue the Celtic uprisings in Spain.	Vercingetorix, the Gaulish chief who rebelled against Caesar, is beheaded in Rome in 46. But there are still risings against Roman rule in Gaul.		In 284 the huge Roman Empire is divided and ruled from two capitals – Rome and Constantinople.	German armies from the north throw out the last Roman Emperor in 476.
			In 220 the Han dynasty collapses in China. In 320 the Gupta Empire is founded in India.	

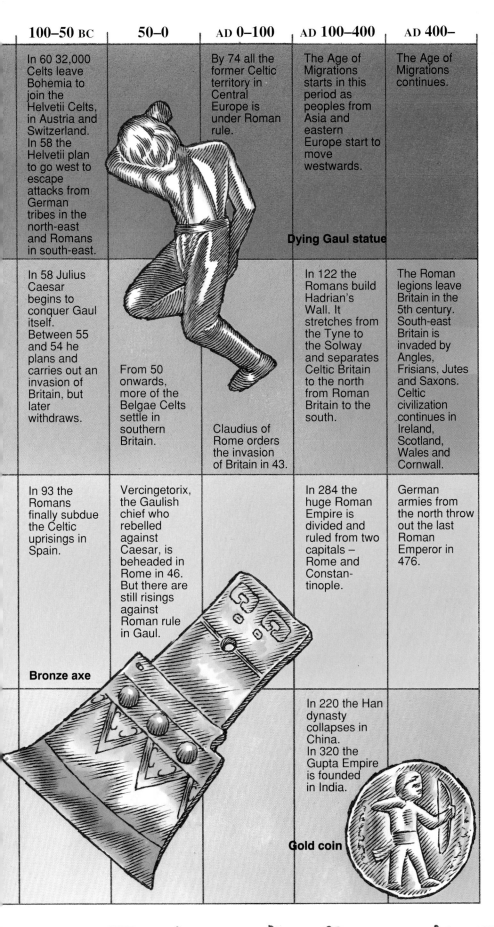

Dying Gaul statue

Bronze axe

Gold coin

THE CELTS AS OTHERS SAW THEM

The Celts never wrote anything about themselves, but people from other civilizations did describe them. Diodorus Siculus who died around 20 BC said they were tall and had blond hair. He also said that noblemen shaved their cheeks, but let their moustaches grow right over their mouths. He added that they were boastful and threatening and said one word when they meant another. Strabo, a Greek geographer who died in AD 21, described the Celts as fond of war, full of high spirits and always ready to do battle. Julius Caesar (100-44 BC) said the same, but added that the Celts soon gave up the fight if the battle started to go against them. Caesar also described the Celts as superstitious people who made human sacrifices to their gods.

Glass bead bracelet

We must remember that these descriptions were written by people who thought their civilizations were better than the Celtic one. This is probably why Caesar said most Britons dressed in animal skins, when in reality British woolen cloth was so good then that it was exported to Rome.

DID·THE CELTS·GROW THEIR·OWN ·FOOD?·

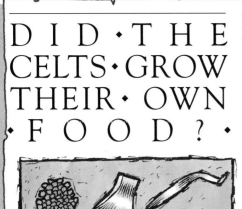

Farming was the main occupation for most of the Celts. With their iron axes, they could clear more of the forests which covered large parts of Europe at that time. The land was then used for growing crops, such as rye, wheat, barley and beans. The barley was used for making beer as well as for flour. Other fields were used as pastures or for growing hay to feed the livestock. This included pigs, which were kept for their meat, and cattle which provided meat and milk. Sheep were also kept for meat, as well as for their wool which was spun and woven into cloth.

CELTIC FIELDS

The Celts liked to farm on soil which was light and easy to plow. Their fields were usually square or oblong and surrounded by a stone wall. They could be plowed in one day with an ard pulled by two oxen. This picture shows part of a reconstruction of a Celtic farm at Butser in Hampshire, England.

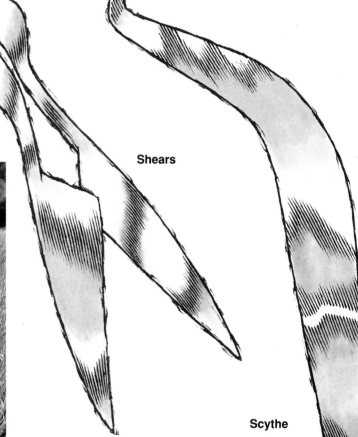

Shears

Scythe

FARMING TOOLS

By La Tene times, Celtic farming tools were very similar to those which were still being used at the beginning of this century. The scythe shown here was fixed to a long wooden handle and used to cut hay. The shears were used to clip wool off the sheep in summer. Another common farming tool was the sickle which was used to harvest the grain.

STORING GRAIN

Harvested grain was often stored in pits. They were about 6 feet deep and lined with wicker or stone. Once filled, the pits were sealed with clay to stop the grain from going moldy.

PROTECTING THE STOCK

In Celtic times, animals such as wolves and bears still lived in most parts of Europe. If they were hungry, they attacked farm animals. Farmers tried to protect their stock by firing iron-tipped arrows like these at any wild animals which attacked them.

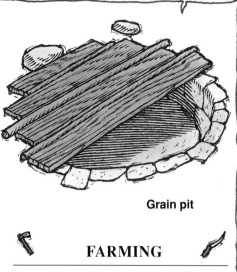

Grain pit

FARMING

When the Roman general Julius Caesar visited Britain with his army in 55 BC, he commented that there were many farms there and also many cattle. He added that the people who lived inland did not grow corn but lived on milk and meat instead. He also said that it was against the law to eat hares, chickens and geese.

HUNTING

Although the Celts grew crops and raised animals for food, hunting was still very important to them. As this bronze model from Spain shows, they were fond of hunting the wild boar which lived in the forests. The Celts usually went hunting on horseback and used spears to kill the animals.

DID·THE CELTS·GO SHOPPING?

The Celts did not go shopping like we do. Instead, they grew their own food and made most of the everyday things they needed. However, luxury goods such as jewelery were bought from specialist craftworkers. Some sold goods at their workshops, but many of them traveled around selling their wares. Some goods were bartered, but others were exchanged for bars of iron and, later, for gold coins.

A BRONZE MIRROR

Roman writers said that the Celts were very proud of their appearance. The men washed their hair with lime water to make it stand up in stiff tufts. They also grew moustaches, but kept the rest of their faces clean-shaven. It seems likely that they would buy mirrors to see how they looked, but this highly decorated example belonged to a woman.

MAKING A TORQUE

A gold torque like the one below was another of the things a Celt would buy, rather than make for himself. This one was made from strands of gold wire. First, eight fine strands were twisted into a thicker strand (1). When eight of these had been made, they were twisted together (2). Finally, two decorated finials were added (3) and the torque was completed.

14

GLASS BRACELETS

By the second half of the third century BC, some of the Celts in southern and central Europe were making bracelets out of glass. As you can see in this photograph, they knew how to make several different colors. They did this by adding small amounts of copper and iron and other minerals to the glass when it was in a molten (liquid) state. Some of the bracelets were smooth and plain, but others had patterns molded into them. Some were also decorated with small amounts of glass in contrasting colors. Many of the glassmakers had their workshops in trading centers and sold their products from there.

CELTIC TOWNS

As the number of Celts grew, some of them settled in communities called oppida. These were like large villages and were often built on the top of hills, where they could be easily defended. Many of the people who lived in the oppida still supported their families by farming. Others made a living by producing goods like the ones shown here. Farmers from surrounding areas brought their surplus food to the oppida to be sold or bartered for other goods. They could then buy other items they wanted from the craftworkers who lived in the oppida.

A BRONZE JUG

For everyday use, the Celts had simple jugs and flagons made from plain pottery or earthenware. However, for special occasions they might have used something more elaborate, such as this wine flagon which is made from bronze. It is one of a pair which was found in France and it is decorated with coral and enamel. Probably only the richest of the Celts could afford something of this quality.

CURRENCY BARS

Iron bars like these have been found at many Celtic sites. They had two possible uses. Before coins came into use, the bars could be used as a form of currency and exchanged for other goods. They could also be kept in readiness for a traveling smith who would melt them down and use them to mend tools and other items.

DID·THE CELTS·HAVE FAMILIES LIKE·OURS?

We do not have very much evidence about the way in which early Celtic families were organized. From later times in Ireland, however, we know that a family was made up of the four generations who were all descended from the same great-grandfather. The land belonged to the whole group and the head of the family was not necessarily the eldest son of the eldest son. Instead, it could be a brother, uncle, cousin or nephew. If there were no male relatives, then a woman could be the head of a family.

MEN AND WOMEN

This bronze head shows a Celtic man wearing a torque around his neck as a symbol of his authority. It tells us that he was probably a warrior, as well as a farmer and the head of his family. To him the family probably meant more than just his wife and children. It probably also included his parents and any single brothers or sisters, but they would all support each other by working together on the farm. Although the man was usually the head of the family, many women seem to have been treated as equals. In some noble families women became rulers and many of them were buried with valuable jewelery. Family ties must have been important as statues from Roman times show defeated Celts killing their wives then themselves, rather than becoming slaves.

CHILDREN

This plaque showing a young girl combing a goddess's hair is one of the very rare images of a Celtic child. Not much is known about them. However, as there was no school, they probably all had to help around the house and the farm as soon as they were able to be useful.

FAMILY PETS

Little models of dogs have been found in archaeological excavations throughout the Celtic world and so it seems likely that they were kept as family pets, as well as being working dogs. The one below is made of bronze and was found in the north of England.

🔩 THE OLD AND POOR ⚷

The Celts looked after people who were old, poor or sick, making sure they had food, clothes and shelter. If these people had no families of their own, then they were looked after within their local community. As early as 300 BC the Celtic tribes in Ireland ran hospitals.

WOMEN'S WORK

Celtic women prepared all the food for their families. This included making butter and cheese, as well as cooking. They also had to grind grain into flour and make bread every day. Another task which kept them busy was making woolen cloth. After the sheep had been clipped, the knots were combed out of the fleece. It was then spun into yarn on a spindle, before being woven into cloth. Wool-combs like these, which are made from bone, have been found by archaeologists on many Celtic sites.

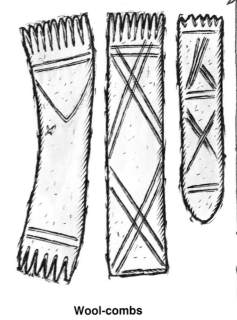

Wool-combs

DID · THE · CELTS · LIVE · IN HOUSES ?

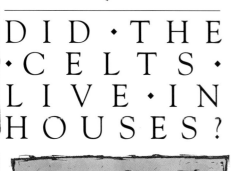

Although no complete houses from Celtic times exist any more, archaeologists have found enough evidence to know what they looked like and to make reconstructions. They know that many of the houses were round in shape, but some were oval, oblong or square. The walls were built of stone or of wattle and daub, depending on what materials were available nearby. The roofs were thatched with straw or reeds. Sometimes the houses were partially underground and connected to each other with narrow passages.

THE HOUSE AT LITTLE BUTSER

This reconstruction of a large Celtic house is at Little Butser in Hampshire, England. Its framework is made from tree trunks and its roof is thatched with straw. The walls are made from a mixture of interwoven twigs and mud, called wattle and daub. The way into the house is through a wooden door under a porch. Some porches also had an outer door to stop sudden drafts blowing into the house and making sparks fly from the fire.

DUN CARLOWAY BROCH

Some of the Celts in Scotland lived in stone towers called brochs. These were circular and had a double wall with a stone staircase running up inside it. This staircase gave access to the living rooms which were built inwards from the inner wall.

INSIDE A CELTIC HOUSE

As this reconstruction shows, a Celtic house had just one big room. The fire burned on a hearth in the middle and provided heat and light. It was also used for cooking. The floor was made of hard-packed mud, but the thatched roof was a great fire risk. This was because there was no chimney and so sparks from the fire could easily set the roof alight.

Wine jug

Wine amphora

 FURNITURE

Archaeologists have not found much evidence for Celtic furniture, but there were possibly wall hangings inside the houses to keep the drafts out. At night people slept on the floor wrapped up in the skins of wild animals such as bears and wolves.

Large dish

COOKING

The Celts did all their cooking over the open fire. Instead of flat-bottomed pans, they had round-bottomed cauldrons like this one. It was held over the flames on an iron tripod.

EATING A MEAL

The Celts sat on the floor to eat their meals. Food was served onto dishes made of wood or earthenware. There were knives but not forks and so some food would be picked up in the fingers. Wine was drunk from small silver goblets, but beer was drunk from wooden tankards.

Cauldron and chain

WHO·WENT TO·WORK·IN THE·CELTIC ·LANDS?·

Unlike people today, most Celts worked for themselves on their own farms. The women and children helped with the farm work. Some Celts probably also had slaves to help them with the heavy work as slave-chains have been found. There were some specialist workers, however, who made things that people could not make for themselves. The most important were the smiths and metalworkers who made tools, weapons, jewelery and items such as cups, bowls and vases. Others included salt miners, potters, woodworkers and traders.

THE SMITH'S FORGE

This reconstruction shows a smith's forge from Celtic times. Here he heated a bar of iron in the fire until it was red hot. Then he put it on the anvil to hammer it into the shape he wanted. He could only do this when the metal was hot and so he had to keep heating it up again.

MINING SALT

At Hallstatt the main salt deposits were underground. To reach them, the salt miners made sloping shafts into the mountainside. Then they dug tunnels into the salt, using bronze-headed picks. Torches like these helped them to see what they were doing in places where there was no daylight.

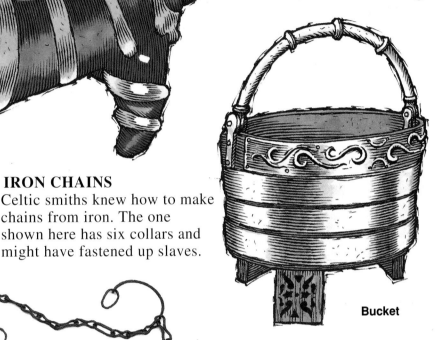

Glass ornament

GLASSWORKERS
Another specialist craft for the Celts was glassmaking. As only a very small amount could be made at a time, it was mostly used for items such as beads and bracelets and for ornaments like this little dog.

IRON CHAINS
Celtic smiths knew how to make chains from iron. The one shown here has six collars and might have fastened up slaves.

Bucket

BRONZEWORKERS
Everyday objects such as buckets and bowls were made from wood. However, for special occasions, the wood was covered with thin sheets of bronze embossed with a pattern. The handle and legs were also made of bronze.

SLAVES

Slaves were important to the Celts in two different ways. First of all, they probably helped with heavy and dirty work around the farms. More importantly, however, slaves could be exchanged for other goods which the Celts wanted. This slave trade became even more important as the Roman Empire increased in size and strength. This was because the Romans relied on slave labor to run the mines and the farms which supported the Empire. Some of these slaves were Celts who had been defeated in battle by the Romans, but others had been sold into slavery. Some of these slaves had been defeated in battle by the Celts and taken prisoner, but others had been captured and made into slaves. They were often exchanged for wine. The Celts were fond of wine, but many of them lived too far north to grow suitable grapes.

WHO · DID THE · CELTS · TRADE · WITH ?

Because their civilization lasted such a long time and covered such a wide area, the Celts traded with many different peoples. The earliest trade was in salt from the mines around Hallstatt to northern Italy and Greece. The salt was used to preserve meat, especially at the end of autumn when many of the farm animals were killed because there was not enough food to keep them all until the spring. Later, goods such as weapons, pottery, slaves, wine, raw materials and craft goods were traded among the different tribes of Celts and also with other peoples. Increasing trade between the Celts and the Romans probably helped the Roman Empire to expand so successfully.

LUXURY GOODS

This silver cup was made in the first century BC. It was probably made in Italy, but it was found in a chieftain's tomb in southern England in 1906. Other luxury items also came from Rome to the homes of rich Celts in Britain in the years before the Roman Conquest. They included bronze and glassware, small statues, and coins which were used as ornaments and pendants.

Some Roman pottery also came to Britain at this time. Some of it was of a very good quality, but a lot of it was a cheap imitation of the original. Many of the imitations were made in southern Gaul and traded with Celtic tribes further north. They were also sent to Britain. Later, potters in southern Britain made their own imitations of Roman pottery and these were traded as far north as Scotland.

ENAMEL WARE

As well as being skilled metalworkers, the Celts knew how to decorate their products with enamel. The most popular color was red, but they also used blue and yellow. This enamel was used on some shields and helmets. It was also used to decorate some of the bronze parts of a horse's harness, such as this bronze plaque which was found in France. It dates from the first or second century BC and was probably made in Britain. Small items like this could easily be taken across the sea and then transported through Europe along one of the many overland routes.

ROMAN AMPHORAE

This photograph shows some of the grave goods which were found in the tomb of a Celtic chieftain in Britain. In the background are four amphorae. These are pottery vessels which were imported from Rome. Most of them were filled with wine (see page 21), but some were filled with fish sauce from the south of Spain.

TRADE ROUTES

As this map shows, the Celts traded goods across most of Europe and around the Mediterranean. Goods were transported by land and by sea. Celtic traders probably also met traders from other parts of the world, as silk from China has been found in some Celtic tombs.

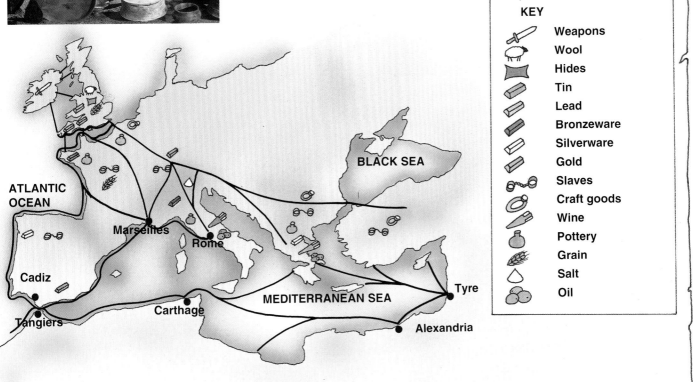

KEY

- Weapons
- Wool
- Hides
- Tin
- Lead
- Bronzeware
- Silverware
- Gold
- Slaves
- Craft goods
- Wine
- Pottery
- Grain
- Salt
- Oil

ATLANTIC OCEAN

BLACK SEA

Marseilles

Rome

Cadiz

Carthage

MEDITERRANEAN SEA

Tyre

Tangiers

Alexandria

Celtic clothes were practical, rather than fashionable. Men wore long woolen trousers, called bracae, and a sleeveless shirt, fastened with brooches. When it was cold, they also wore a cloak which was fastened with a brooch on the shoulder. Women wore a long-skirted gown and also a shawl or cloak for cold weather. They liked bright colors which they obtained from vegetable dyes and they also liked material patterned with squares and stripes.

BROOCHES

The Celts did not have zips and buttons like we do. Instead, both men and women used brooches to fasten their clothing. The most common brooches were called fibulae. As you can see in this photograph, they were rather like a safety-pin. Everyday ones were made from bronze and only had simple patterns. However, special fibulae were often made from gold and decorated with brightly colored enamel or pieces of coral.

JEWELERY

Many Celtic women wore strings of beads around their necks. The beads were usually made of glass. Many of them were plain, but blue beads with a white pattern were also very popular. Some brooches and pins were also worn for decoration, rather than just to fasten clothes together. Finger-rings, toe-rings and bracelets of bronze and gold were also worn by some women.

FOOTWEAR

This workman's shoe was found in the salt mines at Hallstatt. Because it is made of leather, it would normally have rotted away over the centuries, but the salt in the mine preserved it. Most Celts probably wore simple shoes like these, but some trimmed with gold have also been found.

Bronze belt

MAKING CLOTHES

The woman shown below probably made all the clothes that she and her family needed for everyday wear. After spinning the wool into yarn, she colored it with vegetable dyes. She could then weave it into patterned cloth on an upright loom. She cut the clothes from the cloth and sewed them together with a needle made from bone.

A BRONZE BELT

Celtic women usually wore gowns which were long and loose-fitting. They did not have elastic to pull the gowns in at the waist. Instead, they used belts. These were often made of cloth or leather and fastened with a decorated buckle. However, some wealthy women had belts made from bronze, like this one from Switzerland.

HOW WE KNOW

Although plenty of Celtic jewelery has been found, no complete garments have ever been found. This is because cloth soon rots in the ground. However, brooches have sometimes been found with small pieces of cloth still attached to them. To the naked eye, this cloth is usually dull brown in color. When archaeologists analyze it in a laboratory, they can find out what dyes were used to color the yarn before it was woven. These dyes came from plants such as woad, madder and weld. These gave the colors blue, red and yellow. They could also be mixed together to give other types of colors.

WHAT·DID THE·CELTS DO·ON·THEIR HOLIDAYS?

The Celts did not go away on vacations in the way that we do today. Because most of them were farmers, they had to stay at home and look after their crops and animals all year round. However, this did not stop them enjoying themselves with sports and games in their spare time. They also celebrated at least two big religious festivals each year. These were Samhain on 1 November, and Beltane on 1 May. Beltane marked the day when the cattle went out into open grazing. These festivals were celebrated with feasting, drinking, fires and music.

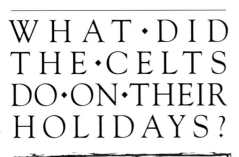

CELTIC FEASTS

A lot of drinking took place at all Celtic feasts. Ordinary people drank beer which they brewed themselves from barley, or mead which was fermented from honey. However, wealthy Celts and chieftains were more likely to celebrate with imported wine. This was often served from special containers, such as this silver cauldron from Gundestrop in Denmark.

The wine was poured into silver cups (see page 22), but mead was usually drunk from drinking horns. As well as drinking a lot, the Celts also ate plenty of meat at their feasts. This included pork and venison, which were roasted on a spit over the fire. When the meat was cooked it was divided up in such a way that the most important people got the best bits.

GAMES OF CHANCE

From the number of playing pieces which have been found in graves and other excavations, it seems that the Celts were quite keen on games of chance. The pieces in this photograph are part of a set of twenty-four. They are made of glass and can be divided by color into four groups of six.

Trumpet

Carnyx

MUSIC AND DANCING

Although there are written descriptions of the Celts enjoying music and dancing, there is very little other evidence for it. Only a few musical instruments have been found, but we know of them from objects like the Gundestrop cauldron which shows men playing carnyxes on one of its panels. Some pottery also shows people dancing.

SAMHAIN AND HALLOWEEN

Samhain was the name for the Celtic New Year. It was celebrated on 1 November and marked the end of the grazing season and the start of the winter. At this time, all the farm animals were gathered together and those which were not needed for breeding in the following spring were killed for food. Because Samhain did not belong to the old year or the new one, it was thought to be a time of magic. Magical armies marched out of caves, while people were able to pass into the world of spirits and then return. The memory of some of this old magic is now celebrated on 31 October as Halloween.

HORSE RIDING

Horses were important to the Celts as a means of getting around, but the Celts probably also rode for pleasure. This pony cap was found in Scotland. The holes are for the pony's ears to stick out of, but the horns were added to the cap later and have nothing to do with it. The cap protected the pony in races.

WHO·DID THE·CELTS WORSHIP?

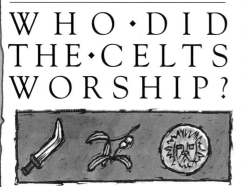

The Celts had many different gods and goddesses. Their religion was tied in closely with nature and their environment, and many gods were associated with streams, trees and stones. Both the Gauls and the Celtic tribes in Britain had religious leaders called Druids. They were like wise men or witchdoctors. They were involved in education and also demanded sacrifices. British Celts who survived the Roman Conquest eventually became Christians.

THE EARLY GODS

One of the best known of the early Celtic gods and goddesses is Epona, the horse goddess. Sometimes she is depicted as a horse's head, as she is in this photograph, but other times she is shown as a woman riding on a horse. Among other things, she was the goddess of fertility and sacrifices to her would help the crops to grow. Another Celtic goddess was Elen who was associated with water and healing. In Christian times some of the springs and wells associated with her were renamed as Saint Helen's wells.

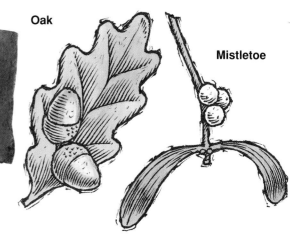

Oak

Mistletoe

SACRED GROVES

The Celts are known to have had some temples, but many of their religious activities took place in sacred groves. These were supervised by the Druids and ordinary people were not allowed to go too close to them. The Roman poet, Lucan, described one which he had seen in France. He said the trees grew so thickly there that the sun could not shine through them. Some trees had been chopped down and carved into rough images of the gods. The most sacred tree was the oak. Mistletoe was also sacred and could only be cut by a Druid with a gold sickle.

ROMANO-BRITISH GODS

When the Romans invaded Britain in AD 43, they tried to relate the local Celtic gods to the gods which they knew. These included Mercury, Mars and Neptune. The Romans built temples to these gods, but they also acknowledged the old Celtic gods in the names of some of the towns they built. For example, they gave the name Aquae Sulis to the city we now call Bath. Sulis was a Celtic goddess and the Roman name meant 'waters of Sulis'. This carving from Bath shows a Roman image of a Celtic god.

CHRISTIAN CELTS

The Celts in Britain became Christians in late Roman times and kept their new religion after the legions left Britain. They celebrated their Christianity with carved crosses such as this one at Monasterboice in County Lough in Ireland. It dates from the tenth century AD.

HEALING

The Celts were superstitious and often made sacrifices if they were ill. However, they also tried to treat their illnesses and injuries as best they could. As well as using herbs and medicines, they had surgeons who performed operations using instruments like these.

THE DRUIDS

The Druids were religious leaders and often political leaders too. They were the wise men of the tribe and spent up to twenty years memorizing all the knowledge they needed to perform their various ceremonies. Two of the most important were Beltane and Samhain. Sometimes the Druids demanded sacrifices. They knew the laws of the tribe and might even make decisions about war.

Surgical instruments and probes

29

DID·CELTS· BELIEVE·IN LIFE·AFTER ·DEATH?·

The Celts believed that when people died they simply moved on to another world where life went on exactly as before. It was sometimes known as the Otherworld and people could also die there. When this happened, the person was then reborn in this world. Because they believed in this kind of life after death, the Celts usually buried their dead with some of their favorite belongings, including jewelery, clothes and other things which would be useful to them in the next life, as well as food.

CHARIOT BURIALS

This photograph shows a Celtic grave which has been excavated in Britain. It is known as a chariot or a cart burial as a chariot was placed in the grave with the body. Sometimes the wheels were taken off the chariot and laid flat and then the body was placed on top of them. The body was usually put on its side in a crouching position. In some chariot graves, the bones of horses, together with the metal pieces of their harnesses, have also been found. However, it seems that the Celts were very practical and usually used old, worn-out chariots and equally worn-out horses for these burials. Most bodies in chariot graves have been buried with weapons such as a sword and several spear heads, as well as some jewelery.

A COUCH FROM A PRINCELY TOMB

The graves of very rich Celts are often known as princely tombs. Some of the best are in central Europe. One in Germany contained this bronze couch on which the body was laid. The tomb was from the sixth century BC and also contained a cart, a cauldron which had held mead, nine drinking horns and nine plates. The man had a quiver of arrows, plus a knife, a gilded belt and shoes, and gold jewelery.

FOOD AND DRINK

Apart from jewelery and weapons, the most usual finds in Celtic tombs relate to either eating or drinking. Many pottery cups, plates and containers, like the ones reconstructed here, have been found in all parts of the Celtic world. One man was buried with no less than 10 gallons of Italian wine, while other people were buried with joints of meat and even cauldrons to cook them in. Archaeologists can analyze the pottery to find out what it contained and where it was made.

Pottery containers

A drinking horn

GRAVE ROBBERS

Gold artifacts are usually the best preserved objects in tombs. Unfortunately people in the past also knew that they had been buried and many of them were stolen. This gold drinking horn is one of a pair which survived to be excavated by archaeologists in Germany.

CELTIC FUNERALS

Because of their belief in another life, the Celts were said to cry at a birth and laugh at a funeral. They thought that the dead people went to the Otherworld for a certain number of years. This meant that everyone would eventually meet up again. However, not all Celts were buried. From the first century BC, many of them were cremated and the remains of their bones were placed in pottery urns. These were sometimes also buried with grave goods to help the person on the way to the next life. When the Celts became Christians, they went back to burying their dead, but they no longer buried any grave goods with them.

· W H O · RULED·THE · C E L T S ?

The Celts were never ruled as one people or an empire. Instead, each tribe had its own leader who was from the noble or warrior class. Sometimes, however, there was a king above this leader and he ruled over several tribes. Apart from nobles and warriors, Celtic society was divided into farmers and learned men. This last group included doctors, Druids, bards and metalworkers.

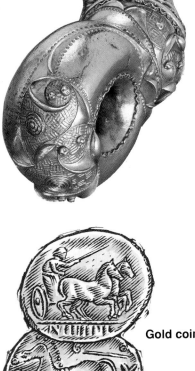

THE SNETTISHAM TORQUE

Torques, or collars, like this one from Snettisham in Norfolk, England, were worn by members of the warrior class. They were usually made of gold or electrum, which was a mixture of gold and silver. They were very valuable and so they were usually melted down and their gold used to make something else if they broke or became old-fashioned.

GOLD COINS

By the second century BC, the Celts had started to use money instead of bartering for the goods they wanted. Their coins were mostly made from gold and each tribe made its own. The name of the tribe's ruler was usually on the coin.

Gold coins

HILL FORTS OR OPPIDA

This is an aerial view of Maiden Castle in Dorset, England. The ditches around it protected the people from their enemies. The houses were built in the open area on top of the hill. In times of danger, the farm animals could be brought into this area to graze. Many hill forts were also trading and craft centers, as well as defensive sites.

🔘 FRIENDS AND FOES 🔘

As the Roman Empire expanded, some Celtic tribes joined together to fight against the Roman legions. However, others welcomed the new Roman rulers and this sometimes led to betrayal among the Celts. For example, in AD 43 King Caratacus of the Catuvellauni in south-east Britain was defeated when he tried to resist the Romans. He fled to Wales and then to the northern British queen, Cartimandua. She betrayed him to the Romans and he was sent into exile.

Warrior-god statue

QUEEN OF THE ICENI

This statue shows Boadicea, or Boudicca, the Celtic queen who ruled the Iceni tribe in eastern England after her husband's death in AD 60. She led her people into revolt against Roman rule. The Iceni attacked the Roman cities of Colchester, London and St Albans before the rebellion was harshly put down.

WARRIOR-GODS

Warriors played an important part in Celtic society. They were usually wealthier than everyone else and were often chosen to rule tribes. This bronze statue from France shows a warrior-god from the second century BC.

None of the early Celts painted pictures. Instead, their artists produced beautifully patterned metalwork using gold, silver and bronze for many different artifacts. Some of these were useful and others were just for ornament. As well as using geometric patterns, they also decorated metal objects with human and animal heads and made little bronze figures of dogs and wild boar. Some of them put colored patterns on metal by using enamels. Later, some Celts carved patterns on memorial stones. Some of their distinctive styles are still used today.

USING GOLD

This wooden cup has been decorated with gold leaf in an openwork design. Some of the gold leaf has been embossed, or raised, to show the pattern more clearly. The cup dates from the fifth century BC and was found in the tomb of a rich man or prince in Germany. The wood had rotted away long ago, but archaeologists had enough evidence to reconstruct it so that a new one fitted into the metalwork which had survived more or less intact. Other gold objects which have survived in tombs include patterned strips of gold which were used to decorate shoes. It is possible that some of the patterns were stamped onto the metal as some of them are repeated several times on one object. This could be done by cutting the pattern in reverse on a die, or a stamp, made of iron and then pressing it onto a sheet of softer metal.

34

AN ORNAMENTAL HELMET

This helmet is from a chieftain's tomb at Ciumesti in Romania. The helmet is made from iron, but the bird of prey on the top is made from bronze. Its wings move up and down as if it were flying. It dates from the third century BC and must have been used only for ceremonies and to show how important its owner was. If it was worn in battle, the bird on top would make it easy to knock the helmet off the owner's head.

ENAMELING

The Celts made red enamel by heating a mixture of quartz glass, lead and cuprite until it melted (1). They then got the object they wanted to decorate (2) and roughened the surfaces which were to be enameled. This made sure that the enamel would stick when it was poured in (3).

FAVORITE PATTERNS

As well as liking geometric designs, the Celts were fond of swirling patterns. Some of these were like the tendrils of plants. Another favorite pattern was the three-legged triskele which is still used as the emblem of the Isle of Man. Some popular animal designs included geese and hares, both of which were thought to be magical.

MAKING CIRCLES

As you can see from the bronze phalera or plaque in this photograph, many Celtic designs were based on circles. These were made with iron compasses. Sometimes the pattern was made straight onto the object. Another way was to make a wax model of the object and put the pattern on that. It was then covered in clay and heated to melt the wax. Molten bronze was then poured into the mold and left to harden.

D I D · T H E · C E L T S · W R I T E B O O K S ?

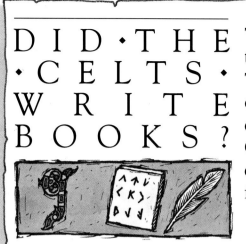

The Druids would not allow the Celts to read or write, but this does not mean that they were not great story-tellers. Their poems, legends and histories were passed on by word of mouth from one generation to the next and were written down when the power of the Druids had collapsed. Later Celts who became Christians made beautiful manuscript copies of the Gospels and other religious works. The most famous are the Book of Kells and the Lindisfarne Gospels.

THE BOOK OF KELLS
This is a page from the Book of Kells which is a hand-written copy of the Gospels. It shows a capital P at the start of a chapter and was made by monks in the eighth century AD. It could take months or even years to produce a book like this.

CELTIC ALPHABETS
Most of our knowledge of Celtic writing comes from inscriptions on stones. The letters had to be easy to carve and so they were made up mostly of straight lines. The alphabet shown below was used mainly in Wales and has a total of 30 different letters. The Ogham alphabet at the bottom of the opposite page has fewer letters. It was used in Ireland and western Britain.

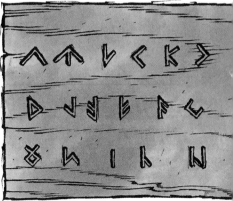

OTHER ALPHABETS

On the continent of Europe, the Celts based their alphabets on those used by the people they had most contact with. Although this inscription from France is in a Celtic language, the letters are based on those used in Massilia (now Marseilles) which was then a Greek colony. Some stones had the same inscription in Celtic and in Latin.

DATES AND CALENDARS

Calendars were one of the few things to be written down by the Druids. One of them has been found in France. It was divided into sixteen columns showing a total of 62 lunar months. These were divided into light halves and dark halves, according to the state of the moon. The days were then numbered and some were labeled as good for starting new ventures.

KING ARTHUR

The legend of King Arthur was first written down by Geoffrey of Monmouth in the twelfth century AD. In the legend Arthur was born at Tintagel in Cornwall. He became King of Britain at the age of fifteen and won many battles. Later he was betrayed by his nephew Modred. Arthur defeated him, but was fatally wounded and taken to the Isle of Avalon to be healed. There his sword was thrown into the water as a sacrifice to the Lady of the Lake. The story was retold many times. This picture is from a fourteenth century version.

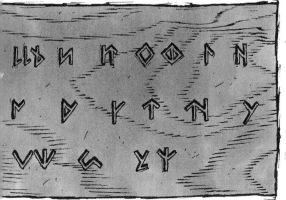

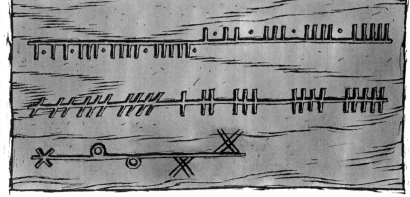

HOW · DID · THE · CELTS TRAVEL ?

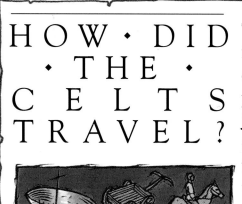

The Celts traveled in many different ways, depending on how far they were going and what they were going for. The earliest of them traveled on foot through the high mountain passes in the Alps, carrying everything they needed for their journey on their backs. In less difficult territory they traveled on horseback or in chariots and wagons. Many Celts lived by the side of lakes and rivers and were able to travel on the water in boats. Others crossed the sea in small ships to trade with neighboring countries.

A FOUR-WHEELED WAGON

Because Celtic wagons and chariots were made mostly from wood, no complete ones have survived. However, archaeologists have found enough evidence in the form of metal fittings and impressions in the soil to make the replica of a wagon shown in this photograph. The wheels had iron tires which were put on when they were hot. As they cooled, they shrank slightly and so held the parts of the wheel firmly together. The wagon was pulled by two horses who were fastened to a wooden yoke at the end of the central pole and controlled by reins.

MAKING A CHARIOT

Chariots were lighter than wagons and were used in battle as well as for transport. However, like the wagons, they were pulled by two horses. In battle they were driven by a charioteer who had a warrior standing beside him. The warrior threw spears and also fought with his sword. The chariot itself was made in several parts. The wheel hub, its spokes and its rim, or felloe, were shaped from wood and fastened together (1). Then the body of the chariot and its pole were made and joined together (2). Finally the sides were added (3) to protect the driver and his passenger.

BOATS

This model of a boat is made from gold and was found in Ireland. It has oars and a mast, so it could be either sailed or rowed. Most Celtic boats were made from wood.

EVIDENCE ON COINS

Although the Celts did not leave any drawings of their horses and chariots, we know a lot about them from engravings on coins such as this one from the first century AD.

3

CORACLES AND MILLSTONES

When the Celts were traveling short distances on water, they often used a coracle. This was a small boat made from a light, wickerwork frame with waterproofed animal skins stretched over it. It was round in shape and paddled with a single oar. Coracles can still be seen occasionally today on the rivers of west Wales. They might also have been used by the Irish saints who went to Cornwall, but legends say they all crossed the sea on millstones!

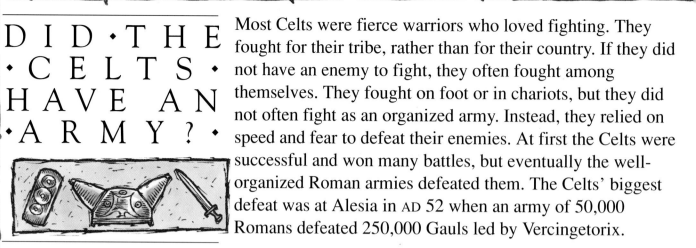

DID·THE ·CELTS· HAVE AN ·ARMY?·

Most Celts were fierce warriors who loved fighting. They fought for their tribe, rather than for their country. If they did not have an enemy to fight, they often fought among themselves. They fought on foot or in chariots, but they did not often fight as an organized army. Instead, they relied on speed and fear to defeat their enemies. At first the Celts were successful and won many battles, but eventually the well-organized Roman armies defeated them. The Celts' biggest defeat was at Alesia in AD 52 when an army of 50,000 Romans defeated 250,000 Gauls led by Vercingetorix.

A CELTIC WARRIOR

This statue of a Celtic warrior from Gaul dates from the first century BC. His body is protected by a tunic made from chain-mail. His sword hangs from a belt around his waist and his cloak fastens on his right shoulder so that he can move his arm easily. He also carries a shield to protect himself, but his head is bare. In earlier times, however, Celtic warriors often went into battle wearing nothing but a gold torque around their necks. They were brave as well as fierce and often fought against much larger armies. If they were defeated in a battle, many of them killed themselves rather than be taken prisoner.

WEAPONS

A Celt's favorite weapon was his sword. It was usually quite long and had a blade made from iron. It was used for slashing at the enemy soldier, rather than stabbing him. When it was not being used, the sword was often protected by a scabbard and suspended by a chain from the warrior's belt. Other weapons included daggers, knives and spears. The Celts sometimes also used battle-axes and bows and arrows. Another popular weapon was the sling-shot, which was used to fire small round stones.

Sword

A HORNED HELMET

This bronze helmet was found in the River Thames in London. It dates from the first century BC and was probably worn on special occasions, rather than in battle. When he was fighting, a warrior was more likely to protect his head with a helmet made of leather.

THE BATTERSEA SHIELD

This shield was also found in the River Thames in London. It is made from a wooden board, covered with a sheet of bronze. The panels on the front are decorated with red enamel. The Battersea shield is flimsy and would not have lasted long in battle. More usual ones were made of wood or thick leather.

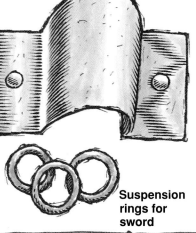

Shield boss or handle

Suspension rings for sword

CELTIC MERCENARIES

Because the Celts enjoyed fighting, many of them went to fight in other people's armies. They even fought for people who had been their enemies in the past. For example, around 474 BC the Celts were fighting against the Etruscans in northern Italy, but around 300 BC they joined forces to fight against the Romans. Other Celtic warriors were recruited into the Macedonian army, while many went to Egypt and to Asia Minor. When Hannibal came from Carthage in 218 BC, the Celts guided his army through the Alps and around 10,000 Celtic warriors joined his army in Gaul to try and defeat the Romans there. However, when Hannibal had to return to Carthage, the Romans soon defeated the Celts.

As the Roman Empire increased in size and strength, it gradually took over most of the Celtic lands and the people in them adopted a Roman way of life. Once Gaul had been defeated, the Romans began to think of adding Britain to their empire. Some tribes accepted this and became Romanized, while others fought against it. In Scotland, Ireland, most of Wales and Cornwall, the Celts managed to maintain much of their old way of life until the time of the Norman Conquest in 1066. Even today, Celtic traditions survive in some areas.

■ Irish advance

□ Angles, Jutes and Saxons

⇨ Irish settlement

⇨ Anglian advance

HADRIAN'S WALL
The Romans hoped to conquer the whole of Britain. When they failed to conquer the tribes in Scotland, however, they built Hadrian's Wall to defend the northern frontier of Roman Britain. It was started in AD 122 and was 74 miles long.

AFTER THE ROMANS
Because there were problems in other parts of the Empire, the Roman legions left Britain at the start of the fifth century AD. Once they had gone, there was a large increase in the number of Angles, Jutes and Saxons invading the country from the east. They settled in the parts of Britain which had been ruled by the Romans, but the Celts remained in Scotland, Wales and the south-west, where they were joined by more Celtic settlers from Ireland.

KING ARTHUR'S ROUND TABLE

In the Great Hall of the castle in Winchester, England, is what is supposed to be the Round Table at which King Arthur sat with his knights. It was possibly made in the thirteenth century AD or even later.

LATE CELTIC JEWELERY

Celtic designs influenced jewelery in Ireland and Scotland for many centuries. Brooches like this were used for fastening cloaks. Some were copied in nineteenth century England when Queen Victoria made them popular.

Brooch

THE CELTIC INHERITANCE

Many of the old Celtic tribes are remembered in place names. For instance, the Parisii gave their name to Paris, while the Belgii gave their name to Belgium. Names of rivers such as the Avon and the Dove in England also come from the old Celtic languages. The languages themselves still survive among people who speak Welsh, Gaelic, Erse, Manx, Cornish and Breton.

CELTIC CHRISTIANITY

After the Romans left, Christianity died out in most of Roman Britain. However, it continued to flourish in Ireland. Communities of monks built monasteries, like this one at Ardmore. Many of them had round towers in which the monks could defend themselves if the monastery was attacked. Eventually monks from Ireland took Christianity back to the western edges of mainland Britain.

·GLOSSARY·

ANGLES People from northern Germany who settled in eastern and northern England in the fifth century AD.

ANVIL A hard block on which the blacksmith hammers hot metal into shape.

ARCHAEOLOGIST Someone who makes a scientific study of the remains of the past.

ARD A simple plow which dug into the soil but could not turn it over.

ARTIFACT An object made by people.

BARD A Celtic poet.

BARLEY A plant which was grown for its grain.

BARTER To trade goods by exchanging them for other goods rather than for money.

CORAL A pinky-red substance used for decoration. It comes from the skeletons of creatures which live in the sea.

CUPRITE A substance which was ground up and used to give the red color to enamel.

DIE A shaped block used to make a pattern on another object.

EMBOSSED A pattern with a raised surface.

FERMENT A chemical reaction in which sugar changes to alcohol.

GROVE A small area of woodland.

HAY Grass which has been cut and dried in the summer and is used to feed the animals over the winter.

JUTES People from north-west Germany who settled in south-east England in the fifth century AD.

LABORATORY A place where objects are studied scientifically.

LEGIONS Another name for the Roman armies.

LUDO A simple game in which the players throw dice to move their playing pieces around a board.

MANUSCRIPT Something which has been written by hand.

MERCENARY Someone who fights for money or other rewards, rather than for a cause he believes in.

MILLSTONE A large heavy stone used for grinding grain into flour.

MONASTERIES Religious communities of men who are called monks.

RECONSTRUCTION An object which has been made to look like the original.

RYE A plant which was grown for its grain.

SACRED Something of great religious importance.

SACRIFICE Offering something of value to please a god. Some sacrifices involved the killing of a person or an animal.

SAXONS People from west Germany who settled in southern England in the fifth century AD.

SCABBARD The sheath in which a sword is kept when it is not being used.

SLING-SHOT A small catapult which is held in the hand to fire small rounded stones.

VENISON Meat which comes from deer.

WICKER Slender twigs which can be woven together. They are usually taken from willow trees.

YOKE A wooden frame to which two animals are attached so they can be worked as a team.

· I N D E X ·